MADE IN THE
U.S.A.

HELICOPTERS

From Start to Finish

Mindi Rose Englart

Photographs by Peter Casolino

BLACKBIRCH®
PRESS

THOMSON
★
GALE™

San Diego • Detroit • New York • San Francisco • Cleveland • New Haven, Conn. • Waterville, Maine • London • Munich

Photo Credits: Cover, all photos © Peter Casolino; except pages 3, 5, 25 © Richard Zellner.

LIBRARY OF CONGRESS CATALOGING-IN-PUBLICATION DATA

Englart, Mindi.
  Helicopters / by Mindi Rose Englart ; photographs by Peter Casolino.
     p. cm. — (Made in the USA series)
Includes index.
Summary: Describes, in text and illustrations, the design, construction, and uses of various types of helicopters.
  ISBN 1-56711-478-4 (hardback : alk. paper)
  1. Helicopters—Juvenile literature. [1. Helicopters.] I. Casolino, Peter, ill. II. Title. III. Series.
TL716.2 .E54 2003
629.133'352—dc21   2002004578

Printed in China
10 9 8 7 6 5 4 3 2 1

Contents

Dedication
To my brother, Eric Marc Englart

Special Thanks
The publisher and the author would like to thank Susan Hitchcock, Robert Araujo, John Soehnlein, Donald Anttila, David Resnick, and the staff at Sikorsky Aircraft for their generous help in putting this project together.

If you would like more information about the company featured in this book, visit www.sikorsky.com

Helicopters are amazing machines. They can hover, or stay, in one place in mid-air. They do not need a runway to take off or to land. They can move up and down or side to side.

More than one million lives have been saved by helicopters landing in hard-to-reach areas. Helicopter emergency workers can rescue people who are stranded in places where airplanes cannot land. But how are helicopters made?

A MEDEVAC helicopter carries and delivers medicine and medical supplies.

The entrance to Sikorsky Aircraft in Stratford, Connecticut.

Sikorsky Aircraft

Sikorsky Aircraft is a large company that makes helicopters. The company has made more than 8,600 helicopters in the past 63 years. The Sikorsky plant in Stratford, Connecticut, is huge! Sikorsky is so big that it has its own fire department, police department, and hospital. It even has its own zip code!

Uses for Helicopters

Most helicopters in the world are used for military purposes. Some helicopters have missiles and rockets attached to them. Others carry large groups of soldiers and equipment. MEDEVAC helicopters deliver important medical supplies and can pick up injured troops.

There are many non-military uses for helicopters, too. They are used to fight wildfires burning in hard-to-reach areas. They deliver supplies to boats and other places where airplanes cannot land. And local news crews use helicopters to fly over highways to see what the traffic is like down below.

The Air Ambulance is one of the most important uses for non-military helicopters. An Air Ambulance carries beds, oxygen, and other equipment found in hospitals. Doctors can even do minor surgery while the helicopter is in the air!

Sikorsky Air Ambulance in action

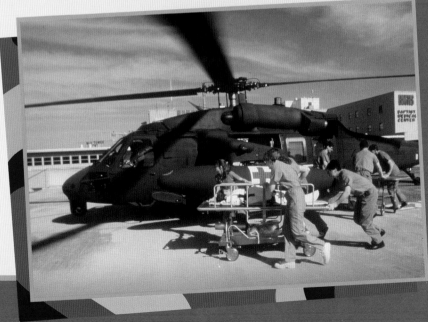

Research and Development

Research and Development (R&D) engineers design new helicopters. They also work to improve older ones. R&D engineers use lots of math and science when they create their designs. They use special computer programs to draw their ideas. These drawings are called schematics. They show each part of the helicopter. Schematics also tell engineers how the parts will fit together. R&D engineers give schematics to pilots and other engineers to find out what they think about their designs.

Research and development engineers use computer programs to design helicopters.

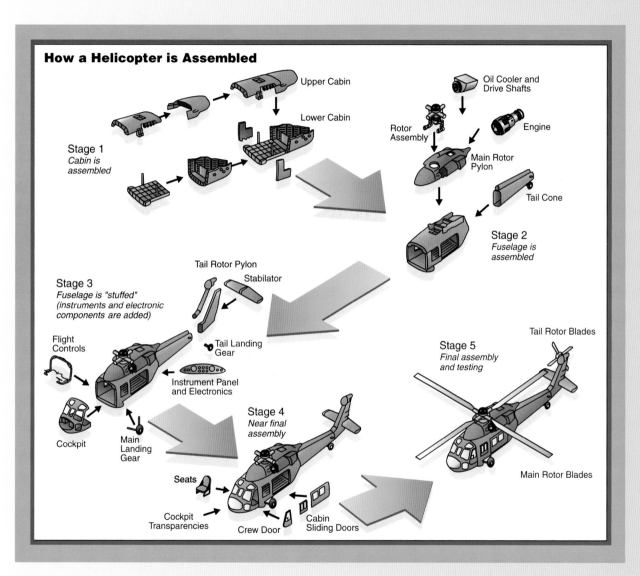

Diagram of UH-60 helicopter

Safer and Stronger

Engineers try to create safe and strong helicopters. For example, a BLACK HAWK helicopter's fuel tank is made of a special self-sealing material. If a bullet is shot into the fuel tank, the hole will automatically close up! BLACK HAWKS have two of each of the most important parts of a helicopter. If one part gets broken, there is another just like it to take over. This is important, especially for the military. If a BLACK HAWK helicopter is attacked, it has a good chance of landing safely.

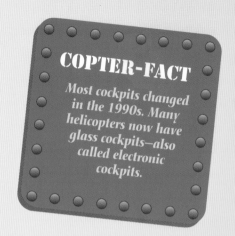

COPTER-FACT

Most cockpits changed in the 1990s. Many helicopters now have glass cockpits—also called electronic cockpits.

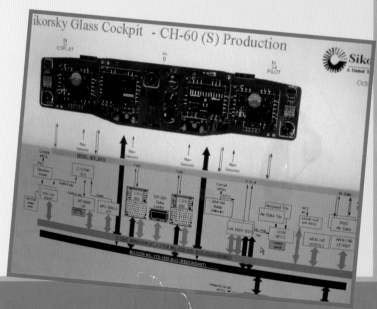

The initial design for a glass cockpit shows how all of the electronic parts will fit together.

Above: *A glass cockpit*

Manufacturing Engineering

A design that has been created and tested by the R&D department then goes to the manufacturing engineering department. Here, a team of engineers builds the helicopter electronically. Manufacturing engineers use special 3-D computer programs. They finish the design with these programs.

The software programs have thousands of drawings of helicopter parts. This allows engineers to see the parts in 3-D. They can rotate helicopter parts on-screen to see how they fit together. They can also tell how a helicopter will look from all angles. When all of the pieces are in place, the computer prints out diagrams.

Manufacturing engineers print lists of all the parts needed to create a helicopter. Workers in the manufacturing department use these diagrams and lists to build the helicopter.

Left: A manufacturing engineer puts a helicopter together on a computer to make sure all of the pieces fit together.

An engineer uses a computer to build a prototype (sample).

Igor Sikorsky

Igor Sikorsky was born in Kiev, Russia, in 1889. He wanted to design an aircraft that could save lives by landing in hard-to-reach areas. In 1910, he tried, but was unable to build the first helicopter in his backyard. He joined the military and studied aviation. He worked on many other projects, but he never stopped thinking about his helicopter idea. In 1939, Igor Sikorsky built the world's first helicopter. He died in 1972, at the age of 83, after a lifetime of achievements and awards.

Above right: *This historic photo shows Igor Sikorsky flying an early helicopter.*
Right: *This statue of Igor Sikorsky sits in the lobby at Sikorsky Aircraft.*

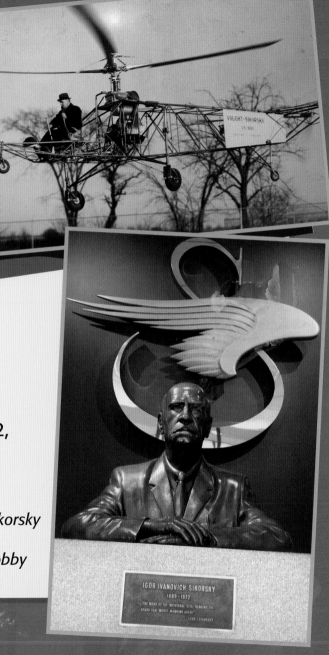

Above: *Igor Sikorsky's office has been left exactly as it was when he died in 1972.*
Left: *Portrait of Igor Sikorsky*

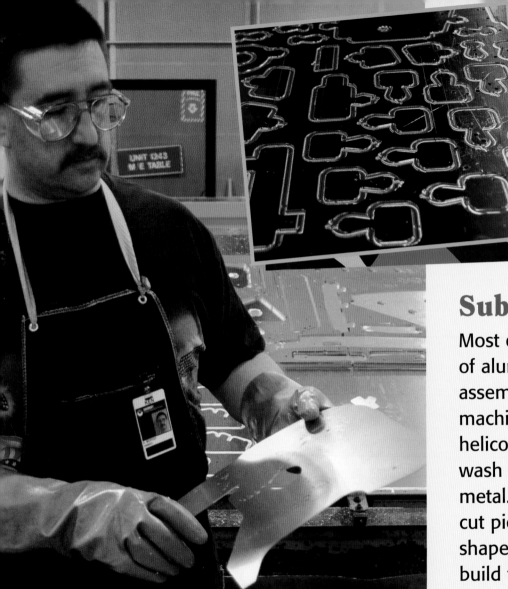

Left above: Many parts are cut from one sheet of metal.
Left below: A worker removes a sheet metal part that has been cut from a larger sheet.
Right: Parts are washed to remove any excess metal chips.

Subassembly

Most of a helicopter is made of aluminum. Workers in the sub-assembly department use special machines to create most of a helicopter's parts. They grind and wash pieces of aluminum and metal. Workers also use lasers to cut pieces of metal into different shapes. These parts are used to build the fuselage—or airframe— of a helicopter. There are millions of parts in a helicopter!

COPTER-FACT

A helicopter blade turns even when the helicopter is on the ground. The blades also get the helicopter off the ground, by moving fast. This is called lift.

Blade Assembly

Sikorsky helicopter blades have 3 main parts. They are the titanium spar, the pocket, and the sheath, which is the front part of the blade. These parts are held together with strong glue. They are put into a mold and covered with a special plate. Then, they are wrapped in plastic and the air is taken out—this is called shrink-wrapping.

Blade parts then enter the autoclave. This is a very large oven that heats blade parts to about 350 degrees. This heating process seals the parts together and makes the blades strong. Once the blades cool, they are sanded.

Opposite above: A blade is assembled before it goes into the autoclave.
Opposite: These titanium parts will be flattened to form blades.
Right: Sanding a blade

Holding It All Together

Major parts of a BLACK HAWK helicopter are held together by rivets. Rivets look like little bolts without threads. They get pressed into the outer covering of a helicopter, called the skin. When rivets are squeezed, they make a very strong connection.

Opposite: Rivet holes are drilled into a helicopter's skin.
Above: Rivets before they are pressed in
Right: A worker finishes the rivet assembly.

Major Assembly

The major assembly department is where parts are laid onto tools. Tools are machines designed by Sikorsky engineers. Subassembly parts are carefully lined up. Then, lots of holes are drilled into specially marked places. Next, workers use rivets to put these parts together. These parts form the bigger pieces of the helicopter.

Helicopter parts are also painted in major assembly. Sometimes they are painted colors that blend into the environment they will fly in. For example, Navy helicopters are painted gray. Some Air Force helicopters are painted camouflage green.

Opposite: *A worker installs a bracket that will support electrical wiring on the aircraft.*
Above: *A worker prepares to paint the inside of a helicopter.*
Right: *Preparing a piece inside the tail cone*

21

Building the Fuselage

Groupings of smaller parts are riveted together to make the fuselage. The fuselage is the structure of the aircraft. The insides of a helicopter are called the cabin. Once the fuselage is ready, a crane lifts it into the final assembly area.

Opposite: *Placing parts onto the (yellow) tool to make the bottom of a fuselage*
Right: *An overhead crane lifts a nearly complete fuselage into the final assembly area.*

The BLACK HAWK

Sikorsky Aircraft has made BLACK HAWK helicopters since 1979. This model is popular because it is powerful and safe. It can lift up to 9,000 pounds, which is about the weight of 2 cars!

It takes about 20,000 hours to build a BLACK HAWK helicopter. Basic BLACK HAWKS are designed to carry an 11-person army squad and 3 other crewmembers. They can fly more than 316 miles without refueling. BLACK HAWKS fly best at around 4,000 feet, but they can fly up to 19,000 feet! Their maximum speed is 184 miles per hour. BLACK HAWKS are 16.8 feet high, 64.8 feet long, and weigh 11,284 pounds.

COPTER-FACT

The U.S. army names all its helicopters after Native American tribes, such as Apache, Comanche, and Black Hawk.

Opposite: BLACK HAWK in flight
Right: BLACK HAWKS have worked out well for the U.S. military.

Final Assembly

Final assembly is where workers put parts inside the fuselage. This is called "stuffing" the fuselage. Workers put in plumbing, fuel systems, windows, and communications systems. They install seats and the equipment that helps pilots navigate, or map, their flights. The engine and landing gear are also installed at this stage.

Opposite: The final assembly area is one big, open space.
Above: A mostly assembled rotor hub. The blades will be attached to the rotor hub at a later stage.

Flight Operations

Flight operations is a helicopter's last stop. Here, a few final steps are completed before a helicopter is ready for a customer. After the fuselage is stuffed, the nearly finished product is rolled out into the hangar, or huge garage. The helicopter is filled with fuel. Then, the rotor and blades are attached. The rotor is the part of the helicopter that spins the blades. The helicopter is then ready for a flight test.

Left: *A fully assembled BLACK HAWK is ready for a test flight.* **Opposite:** *A BLACK HAWK is towed into a hangar.*

29

Pilots practice by using a flight simulator at Sikorsky Aircraft.

A flight test is when a trained pilot flies the helicopter for the first time. He or she tests all controls to make sure they work. After a flight test, workers prepare the helicopter for shipping. Some helicopters are shipped by boat. Certain parts—like the main rotor and blades—are taken off to save space. Then, the helicopter is shrink-wrapped in plastic. This way it won't be damaged by salt from ocean spray. Sometimes Sikorsky delivers new helicopters from a nearby airport.

How Much?

Helicopters can be very expensive. BLACK HAWKS helicopters can cost more than $10 million—and that's just a basic model! Special features can cost much more. Helicopters do so much work, though, that they really are inexpensive for the jobs they can do. Customers also need to put in their requests early—it takes about 2 years to receive an ordered helicopter!

BLACK HAWKS cost millions of dollars.

Glossary

Cockpit Where the pilot sits to fly an aircraft

Fuselage The frame of the helicopter—without inside parts

Glass cockpit Electronic controls in the cockpit

Hangar Very large storage garage for helicopters

Tools In this case, machines built to manufacture helicopters

For More Information

Books

Baysura, Kelly. *Helicopters: Flying Machines.* Vero Beach, FL: The Rourke Book Company, 2001.

Holden, Henry M. *Black Hawk Helicopter.* Berkeley Heights, NJ: Enslow Publishers, 2001.

Website

Sikorsky Aircraft   www.sikorsky.com

Index